HAPPY NATIVES

HAPPY NATIVES

2003 TOUR

3–5 July
Graham College
Grahamstown Festival

8 July–2 August
Baxter Theatre
Cape Town

5–30 August
Theatre On The Square
Johannesburg

2–14 September
Elizabeth Sneddon Theatre
Durban

18–22 September
Hilton Festival

23–26 September
Hexagon Theatre
Pietermaritzburg

The world tour continues from October 2003

HAPPY NATIVES

BY GREIG COETZEE

The play was first presented by B&R Productions in associastion with
Soho Theatre at the Edinburgh Festival Assembly Rooms, August 2002

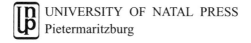
UNIVERSITY OF NATAL PRESS
Pietermaritzburg

Published by University of Natal Press
Private Bag X01
Scottsville 3209
South Africa
E-mail: books@nu.ac.za
Website: www.unpress.co.za

© B&R Productions Limited

All rights reserved. No part of this publication may be reproduced or transmitted in any form or by any means, electronic or mechanical including photocopying, recording or any information storage or retrieval system, without prior permission in writing from the publishers.

ISBN 1-86914-033-8

Cover photograph: Simon Annand
Cover design: Anthony Cuerden

The Producer of Happy Natives wishes to acknowledge financial support received from the Theatre Investment Fund, a registered charity, which invests in many commercial productions, runs workshops for new producers and raises money for the commercial theatre. If you love the Theatre and wish to promote its future, please consider making a gift to the Fund.
For further information regarding the Fund and its activities, please contact:-
Chief Executive, Theatre Investment Fund Limited, 32 Rose Street, London, WC2E 9ET. Telephone: 020 7557 6737

Printed and bound by Interpak Books, Pietermaritzburg

PREFACE

Happy Natives began as a facetious comment during the Edinburgh Fringe 2000 – a response to my growing concern that theatre from Africa presented outside of Africa seemed to follow one or more of three themes: 'wretchedness', 'triumph over adversity' or 'happy dancing natives'. While I do not dispute the validity and relevance of these stories (my own piece *White Men with Weapons* is a tale of wretchedness), it is unfortunate that they appear to overwhelm the many other stories to be told about a very complex continent.

And so, when Ian Ross and Christine Harmar-Brown approached me during August 2000, these were the thoughts I was playing with. Looking back, it was a very fortunate meeting because, without Christine's input and her role as a very level-headed devil's advocate, I think the script would have been a humourless diatribe.

As I was also exploring the relationship between Africa and the world-view of Africa, it helped enormously to have a 'non-African' as a dramaturg and director. As part of the process, Christine came out to South Africa and spent some time seeing the country away from the usual tourist traps. As a writer, this was invaluable because I was suddenly seeing my own country through new eyes.

Greig Coetzee

B&R PRODUCTIONS

Launched in 1999, B&R Productions' most recent shows include *Blessings*; a national tour of *Goodbye Gilbert Harding* presented in association with New Vic Workshop, both first productions of new writing; and a national tour of Tom Stoppard's *The Real Thing* in association with Act Productions, Bristol Old Vic and Theatre Royal Plymouth. Furthering our aim to combine presentations of revived and contemporary classics with the development of new writing, we are delighted to be presenting this production of *Happy Natives* in association with Soho Theatre. The production world premiered at last year's Edinburgh Fringe Festival and is currently on a world tour. The company is already working with Greig Coetzee on the development of his latest play, 10 X 8.

Company Director/Executive Producer   Ian Ross
Company Director/Literary Development   Christine Harmar-Brown
Associate Producer   Alison Carney

SOHO THEATRE

Situated in the very heart of London's West End, Soho Theatre and Writers' Centre is home to the pioneering Soho Theatre Company. The venue was a Lottery success story when it opened in 2000 and quickly established itself as one of London's key producing theatres.

'a glittering new theatre in Dean Street' – *The Times*

Soho is passionate in its commitment to new writing, producing a year-round programme of bold, original and accessible new plays – many of them from first-time playwrights.

'a foundry for new talents . . . one of the country's leading producers of new writing' – *Standard*

Soho aims to be the first port of call for the emerging writer and is the only theatre to combine the process of production with the process of development. The unique

Writers' Centre invites writers at any stage of their career to submit scripts and receives, reads and reports on over 2 000 per year. In addition to the national Verity Bargate Award – a competition aimed at new writers – it runs an extensive series of programmes from the innovative Under 11's Scheme, Young Writers' Group (14–25s) and Westminster Prize (encouraging local writers) to a comprehensive Workshop Programme and Writers' Attachment Scheme working to develop writers not just in the theatre but also for radio, TV and film.

'a creative hotbed . . . not only the making of theatre but the cradle for new screenplay and television scripts' – *The Times*

Contemporary, comfortable, air-conditioned and accessible, the Soho Theatre is busy from early morning to late at night. Alongside the production of new plays, it is also an intimate venue to see leading comedians from the UK and US in an eclectic programme, mixing emerging new talent with established names. Soho Theatre is home to Café Lazeez, serving delicious Indian fusion dishes downstairs or, upstairs, a lively, late bar with a 1am licence.

'London's coolest theatre by a mile' – *Midweek*

Soho Theatre Company is developing its work outside of the building, producing in Edinburgh and on tour in the UK whilst expanding the scope of its work with writers. It hosts the annual Soho Writers' Festival – now in its third year which brings together innovative practitioners from the creative industries, with writers working in theatre, film, TV, radio, literature and poetry. Our programme aims to challenge, entertain and inspire writers and audiences from all backgrounds.

Soho Theatre and Writers' Centre, 21 Dean Street, London W1D 3NE
Admin: 020 7287 5060 Fax: 020 7287 5061 Box Office: 020 7478 0100

Director	Christine Harmar-Brown and Mark Rayment
Designer	Emma Donovan
Lighting Designer	Flick Ansell
Sound Designer	Gregg R. Fisher
Movement Coach	Gerry Zuccarrello
Dialect Coach	Jan Haydn Rowles
Production Manager	Dean Pitman
Stage Manager	Jane Robinson
Publicity & Marketing	Illa Thompson
Set Built by	TBC
Set Construction	Dean Pitman, William Malinga and Promise Ndawose

We would like to thank Janet Suzman, Sarahleigh Castelyn and James Ngcobo for their support. Special thanks goes to The Performing Arts Administration, University of the Witwatersrand; Linda Steenkamp, Sure Travel Management; and Jill Lamb, Rondebosch Guest Cottages.

CHRISTINE HARMAR-BROWN (Director)
Following a freelance career in theatre as a director of new writing, working for companies such as Paines Plough, Soho Theatre Company and with The Royal Court Young People's Theatre, Christine moved to television to work as a script editor on *Casualty* for two series and then joined La Plante Productions to work for Lynda La Plante as Head of Development.

As well as managing B&R's literary department, developing and identifying new writers and commissioning new plays for production, Christine is now writing full time with both stage and television dramas in development. In addition, she continues to direct for the theatre and to run various writers' workshops for companies such as Soho Theatre and Sgrpt Cymru and for non-theatre organisations such as CAST (an educational support programme for women recovering from addiction, mental illness and for women ex-prisoners).

MARK RAYMENT (Director)
Recent Theatre: Canadian premiere of Alan Ayckbourn's *Things We Do For Love* (Stagewest, Toronto with Sharon Maughan); Neil Simon's *The Sunshine Boys* (National Tour with Ron Moody and Brian Murphy).

Other Theatre in London: Alan Ayckbourn's *Comic Potential* (Lyric Theatre) and *Things We Do For Love* at The Duchess Theatre (with Belinda Lang); *Heritage* by Stephen Churchett at Hampstead Theatre (with George Cole, Gwen Taylor and Tim Piggot Smith); Frank Marcus' *The Killing of Sister George* at Ambassadors Theatre (with Miriam Margoyles); *Deceptions* by Paul Wheeler (with Anna Cartaret and Jamie Glover); Enid Bagnold's *The Chalk Garden* (with Constance Cummings, Robert Fleyming and Jean Marsh); *Tide* (with Susannah York and Brendan Coyle) for The Kings Head Theatre; Assistant to Simon Gray on *Hidden Laughter* (with Felicity Kendal and Peter Barkworth).

Also: John Godber's *Bouncers*, Colchester; national tours of *Hidden Laughter* (with Jan Harvey), Alan Ayckbourn's *Time of My Life* (with Anna Cartaret and Gareth Hunt) and *Things We Do For Love* (with Belinda Lang); *Strip Poker*, Chelmsford; Ronald Harwood's *The Dresser*; Ibsen's *Ghosts*, Wokingham Theatre; co-director on *Kander* and Ebb's *Chicago*, Denise Deegan's *Daisy Pulls it Off* and David Wood's *Tickle*, all for The Wilde Theatre, Bracknell. For the Hexagon Theatre, Reading, Mark directed and designed a cast of 100 in Lionel Bart's *Oliver* and co-directed Jerry Herman's *Hello Dolly* and Alan Parker's *Bugs Malone*.

Pantomimes: Wrote and directed, *Aladdin* (Palace Theatre, Redditch); *The Sleeping Beauty*; *Jack and the Beanstalk*; and *Aladdin* for London Productions (featuring Wayne Sleep, Peggy Mount, Trevor Bannister, Wendy Craig, June Brown, Kathy Staff and Louise English).

Workshop: *Holliday*, a play about Billie Holliday, for the Really Useful Group, London.

Mark directed Oscar Wilde's *Lady Windermere's Fan* for the Oxford School of Drama at the Cockpit Theatre, London and is also Guest Tutor of drama at Line Theatre Arts, Surrey.

GREIG COETZEE

Since leaving teaching at the end of 1995, Greig has been active as a playwright, director and performer. He has been involved in a total of thirteen productions since then, eleven of which he wrote or co-wrote.

He performed his first play, *White Men with Weapons*, in theatres all over South Africa. This production also formed part of the Woza Africa: After Apartheid Festival in July 1997 at the Lincoln Center in New York. During 1998 the play was performed by invitation in Belgium, Holland, Australia and Singapore. Since then, Greig has been back to Europe a number of times to work on other projects as a writer and performer. These projects include two commissions to write plays for the Internationale Nieuwe Scene (a Belgian theatre company), as well as a second commission for B&R Productions.

He has written a number of other plays including *The Blue Period of Milton van der Spuy*, *Breasts – A Play about Men* and *Seeing Red*. His work has received numerous provincial and national South African Awards. At the Edinburgh Fringe 2000, he received The Stage Award for Best Actor on the Edinburgh Fringe and a Scotsman Fringe First Award.

SELLO SEBOTSANE

Whilst training at Pretoria Technicon, Sello appeared in a variety of productions, including *Salome*, *The Secret Diary of Adrian Mole*, *Guys & Dolls* and *Woza Albert*, for which he won the Glass Crown Best Actor Award.

Since graduating in 1993, Sello's professional credits include:

Theatre: *Sleeping Beauty*, *Crashing the Night*, *A Streetcar Named Desire*, *Long Wait*, *Big Dada* for which he was nominated the 2001 Fleur de Cup Best Actor Award, *A Woman and Her Words*, *Buddy Holly* and *Scribble*. He has also toured with *Happy Natives* throughout the UK, and at the Africalia Festival in Belgium.

Industrial Theatre: *Unembeza* for which he won the Gold Loerie Award, *MTN New Drums of Africa*, *Idols South Africa* and *Izingwenyazase RBM*.

Films: *Jock of the Bushveld*, *Panic Mechanic*, *Ernest Goes to Africa* and *Tarzan*.

TV: *SOS*, *Scoop Scoombie*, *Egoli*, *Viva*, *Hidden City*, *Madam and Eve* and *It's a Funny Country*.

Sello is also an active voice-over artist.

EMMA DONOVAN (Designer)

Emma graduated in Theatre Design from Nottingham Trent University and has designed a variety of opera, dance, drama and film in the last ten years.

Recent designs include: *Beautiful Thing* (Jonathan Harvey), Nottingham Playhouse and national tour; *Death of a Salesman* (Arthur Miller), Haymarket Theatre, Leicester; *Les Contes D'Hoffman* (Offenbach), European tour and a charity benefit of Afghan refugees at the Bridewell Theatre.

Current and future projects include: *Eugene Onegin* (Tchaikovsky), Scottish Opera Go Round; *Plague of Innocence* (Noel Grieg) with RJC Dance Co.; *The Witches* (Roald Dahl); and *West Side Story*, all for the Haymarket Theatre, Leicester.

FLICK ANSELL (Lighting Designer)

Flick's most recent credits include: Chelsea Theatre's *Exclude Me*; London Bubble's *Panto* at Greenwich Theatre; *Ali Baba and the Forty Thieves*, *The Triumph of Life* and *Ruthless* at Stratford Circus One; The Royal National Theatre's *The Good Woman of Setzuan*; Kompany Malahki's *Fuzion* at BAC; *Big Bad Duvet Terror* and *Hideaway* for Quiconque Theatre Company; The Royal Academy of Music's *Rape of Lucretia* (2000) and *Incoronazione di Poppea* (2002); Southwark Playhouse's *The Glass Slipper*; The Clod Ensembles' *Silver Swan* at BAC and *In Flame* at The Bush Theatre; for Kali Theatre Company *River on Fire* and *Sock 'em with Honey*. Flick has worked as Associate Lighting Designer for the Royal National Theatre's *Threepenny Opera* and Bill Kenwrights' *Star Quality* at The Apollo, Shaftesbury Avenue.

See www.flickansell.com <http://www.flickansell.com> for portfolio.

GREGG R. FISHER (Sound Design/Composer)

Gregg recently moved to London from the United States. He trained at Central (MA, Sound Design/Music for Theatre) and in music composition with Nicholas D'Angelo, Alan Oldfield, Will Bottje and at the Bregman Electronic Music Center.

Most recently, he has designed for: *The Stoning* (BAC); *Auntie and Me* (Edinburgh); *Wild Orchids* (AD, Chichester); *The Lucky Ones* (Hampstead); *The Promise* (Tricycle); *London My Lover* (ICA), *Einstein's Eyes* (CPT); *Bus Stop* (Quay); *Peace for Our Time* (Cockpit); *Summer* (L&U); *Untitled* (Circus Space), and *Hystery* (Embassy Studio).

The performance of this play requires one white and one black performer. Each performer plays a number of characters. The characters are all South African.

Black performer: Mto, a black man, early thirties
Prudence, a black woman, late fifties
Xaba, a black man, late forties

White performer: Kenneth, a white man, early thirties
Chenaye, a white woman, late thirties
Jimmy, a white man, mid-thirties
Patel, an Indian man, about sixty
Policeman, white

ACT ONE

SCENE ONE
A stage

It is the final scene of a play written by Mto, inspired by his father's experience as a guerrilla soldier. Throughout this scene the white performer provides vocal support, but is unseen. The black actor is onstage as Mto performing his play. In the dark we hear a toyi-toyi (a militant chant used during street protests, etc.) with Mto leading and the white performer providing the underlying chant of 'Hhayi! Hhayi, hhayi!!' The lights grow as Mto continues the toyi-toyi, listing the names of struggle heroes like Mandela and Sisulu, and then switches to the derisory mention of apartheid leaders, like Magnus Malan, accompanied by the white performer chanting 'Voetsek! Voetsek, voetsek!' The toyi-toyi ends on a loud 'Bopha' from Mto.

WHITE PERFORMER (*Off*)   iAfrica!

MTO   Mayibuye!

WHITE PERFORMER (*Off*)   Mayibuye!

MTO   iAfrica!

Both performers then sing:

Sukumani, nansi imikhonto, isikhathi sesifikile (Rise up, here are the spears, the time has come).
Dubulani zonk' izitha zethu, isikhathi sesifikile (Shoot all our enemies, the time has come).
Sizonqoba nangemikhonto, sizonqoba nangezibhamu (We will conquer with spears and guns).
Dubulani zonk' izitha zethu, isikhathi sesifikile (Shoot all our enemies, the time has come).

The white performer continues humming the melody, fading to nothing underneath the following speech.

MTO   These were the songs of my father. My father, a son of Africa, land of my people. I can remember him as a wasted life. I can remember him as another faceless black victim crushed by the boot of the oppressor. I can remember him as the father who disappeared into the night. The father who crossed the border. The father we never saw again. But I won't. Instead, I remember him as a man who fought for a dream. A dream for freedom. A dream for crossing a river when you cannot swim. A dream for flying over mountains when you have no wings. I must remember him as a lion. A lion who stared into the darkness and fought for the light of a new dawn.

WHITE PERFORMER (*Off*)   Amandla!

BOTH   Awethu!

SCENE TWO

Backstage area

Backstage after the performance of Mto's play.

KENNETH   Mto! China! That was fucking brilliant! Your best performance ever, broer. The sort of stuff I've said you should be doing all along. What can I say? It rocks.

MTO   Kenneth? Is it Kenneth?

KENNETH   Yes, of course it's Kenneth. You're such a shit – always the funny guy. We're like brothers and here you're all: 'Is it Kenneth?' What's this, Mto? We're old China's, man.

MTO   No, it's just . . . you look different.

KENNETH   Beard's gone. That's it. I had a little beard before. And sideburns. Must have thrown you for a moment. People don't recognise me since I changed the look.

MTO   What the hell is that on your eyebrow? A spider bite?

KENNETH   It's a piercing. For an eyebrow ring. Just a bit inflamed. Had it done in London.

MTO   I haven't seen you since we did that corporate theatre piece to launch the new Mercedes.

KENNETH   Oh ja! At Sun City, hey, remember Mto?

MTO   How could I forget?

KENNETH   Hey, you did get paid?

MTO   Eventually.

A pause.

KENNETH   So, you finally wrote it, hey?

MTO   Yes.

KENNETH   Your father actually was a freedom fighter, wasn't he?

MTO   A guerrilla, yes.

KENNETH   Went into exile in the sixties.

MTO   It was '78.

KENNETH   One of the heroes of the struggle. Didn't he die attacking a military base? Like single-handed or something?

MTO   We're not sure. He was detained, went into exile, next thing we knew he was dead. He was on the run a lot, underground. We were never told where he was. For our own safety, the less we knew the better. He didn't want to involve us. So, have you been writing? Last thing I remember you were writing that play about bushmen and socialism.

KENNETH   Oh ja, that. The dialectic dialogue between Karl Marx and a bushman. The world's only true socialists, the bushmen. No concept of ownership or possessions. We have so much to learn from them.

MTO   So, when does it open?

KENNETH   No, I've got beyond all that arty student shit. Anyway, enough about me. There's someone I want you to meet. Chenaye! This is Mto. Mto, Chenaye de Villiers.

Kenneth becomes Chenaye.

CHENAYE   Hi.

MTO   Pleased to meet you Chenaye. What do you do?

CHENAYE   I'm a producer. My company is Electric Zebra.

MTO   Electric Zebra?

CHENAYE   Yes, the marketing company. In Jo'burg. And you are amazing. I'm speechless. Those rhythms! Those harmonies! Makes me proud to be African. What can I say? Except, work with us.

MTO   What?

CHENAYE   Kenneth and I are pitching for a corporate theatre piece. It's a government project. We'd like you to come on board. As a partner.

MTO   A partner?

CHENAYE   The government are putting big money into a 'Sell South Africa Campaign'. Part of the brief is a corporate theatre piece for foreign investors.

MTO   What's it about?

CHENAYE   At this stage, I'm seeing one nation, many cultures. I'm seeing natural heritage. I'm seeing human wealth and diversity. And I'm seeing us packaging this into something the global market will jump to invest in.

MTO   So we're talking very 'Rainbow Nation'.

CHENAYE   No, I'm seeing life beyond the rainbow. I'm a South African, just like you, and let's face it: the honeymoon's over. Every newspaper is full of stories about yesterday's heroes being exposed for corruption.

MTO   So what are you saying?

CHENAYE   I'm saying: that's no reason for afro-pessimism. Look at your play. Your father was a hero we can all believe in. Some people choose darkness, some people choose sunshine. There's an idea to play with, Kenneth. Sunshine. 'Attract the warm rays of investment to chase the clouds away for the dawn of the African Renaissance.'

MTO   Have you got funding?

CHENAYE   The budgets are still pending at this stage. A few variables to deal with. Everything is subject to the time-line, which has yet to be concretised. But Kenneth can discuss that further with you. Mto, it's been fabulous meeting you. I'm so excited, delirious in fact, but I must rush. Got some clients waiting. Kenneth, you'll explain everything. Call me when you've got something to show me. Mto, hopefully I'll see you soon.

Chenaye becomes Kenneth.

MTO   So? How much?

KENNETH   Look, we're talking speculative at the moment. But Mto, this is the big league. Electric Zebra are a happening company. Half the board were once political exiles, good struggle credentials, right in there with the government. We're talking serious money here. Big machas.

MTO   Kenneth, I don't know . . .

KENNETH   Look, I'm back from England just to do this.

MTO   England?

KENNETH   For sure! I'm on the verge of opening an office in London.

MTO   Shit, so you're doing well there?

KENNETH   Fully broer! They're lapping me up, lapping me up. They know us South Africans work for our money. No welfare safety net to catch us. Sink or swim. Get with the programme or get off the bus. I'm out here networking at the moment.

MTO   Oh, your working visa expired?

KENNETH   Well yes, but that's not why I'm back. The sun. The surf. I'm a Durban boy – need waves, broer.

MTO   Look Kenneth, nice to see you again, thanks for the offer, but this all sounds a bit borderline. I need cash now – can't afford to put time into a project that might go nowhere. I'm buying a house here in Durban.

KENNETH   'What? Me? Recession? No way!' A homeowner!

MTO   A homeowner with loan repayments, which is why I can't afford to stuff around.

KENNETH   Hey Mto, then you need this too. Come on, how many people did you have in that audience? Twenty? Twenty-five? The audience has gone, Mto. Moved to Perth. Straight theatre's dead, broer, dead. You want to run with the lions, you can't piss like a kitten. You need this. I need this. Us Durban boys, we got to stick together, China. Come, it's a few weeks, and if we pull it off, we're there like a bear. Going like a Boeing.

A pause.

MTO   OK, OK.

KENNETH   That's my boytjie!

MTO   But if I smell any of your old bullshit at any point, you can count me out.

KENNETH   You won't regret it. Hey, we can rehearse at your new place.

MTO   It's a bit small, Kenneth. It's just a little place in Woodlands.

KENNETH   The suburbs! We can use the backyard.

MTO   Well, I'm not sure, you know, the neighbours might . . .

KENNETH   Come on, this is Africa! Sunny skies. Who needs a rehearsal room?

MTO   And it costs nothing, hey?

KENNETH   Look, I'd use my place. It's just, I'm back with my folks, temporarily. Like I said, been in London for two years. My money's all tied up. Offshore.

MTO   OK, fine, we can use my backyard.

KENNETH   So. Woodlands, hey! Not a township boy any more. Stepping up to the suburbs.

SCENE THREE

A backyard

Mto is in the yard of his newly acquired house. He is looking around, peering through windows, picking up a handful of earth, taking in the reality of owning something this big. He has a box of things he has brought, apparently for the house. He picks it up as if to go off with it. Jimmy appears behind him. He has a gun. He moves with the stealth and expertise of someone trained in bush warfare.

JIMMY   Don't move. Do anything quickly – I'll shoot.

Mto does as Jimmy says but then reaches for his pocket.

JIMMY   Stop! Keep your hands where I can see them.

MTO   Take everything. I haven't seen your face so I can't identify you. Just don't shoot me. It's the blue Ford, parked outside. Take it.

JIMMY   I don't want your getaway car. Where are the others?

MTO   What?

JIMMY   You buggers always work in groups. Are they already in the house?

MTO   I don't know who you're talking about.

JIMMY   The other bloody skebengas.

MTO   These are my things. Really.

JIMMY   So what are you doing creeping around this house?

MTO   It's my house.

JIMMY   Bullshit. I saw you jump the fence to get in.

MTO   I'm waiting for the estate agent. She's going to meet me here with the keys.

JIMMY   Oh ja? So, who did you buy it from? What was his name?

MTO   Rush . . . something. Rushbrooke. A man called Rushbrooke.

JIMMY   OK. So what does he look like?

MTO   I never met him, it was through an agency. They told me he's British. He's left. That's why I'm waiting for the agent to bring me the key.

Jimmy walks across. Keeping the gun trained on Mto, he looks into the box.

JIMMY   What's this?

MTO   A post-box.

JIMMY   I can see that, but if this is your house, why would you bring a post-box? Hey? The Rushbrookes left their one behind.

MTO It looks like a little bus.

JIMMY It is a bus. It's a London bus. Scale model. Collector's item.

MTO I want a post-box that looks like a post-box.

Jimmy notices that he's still got the gun trained on Mto. He slips it back into its holster and shoots out his arm, hand extended, unwittingly giving Mto a fright.

JIMMY Jimmy.

MTO What?

JIMMY Jimmy Louw. I'm your neighbour. Welcome to Woodlands.

They shake hands. A pause.

JIMMY Well, what's your name?

MTO Mto. Mto Cele.

JIMMY Right. Well, Mto . . . if you need anything, I'm right here. We're next door neighbours.

MTO Next door neighbours?

JIMMY I'm a stone's throw away. Not that I want you to throw stones at me.

MTO That's a big gun you got there.

JIMMY This house has been broken into a few times since the Rushbrookes left. I told them I'd keep an eye on the place. There's a squatter camp not far from here. And you are . . . a stranger, so I thought, you know . . .

MTO The place is empty. There's nothing to steal.

JIMMY Oh you'd be surprised. Light fittings, window frames, kitchen sink . . . these people are desperate. They take anything . . . squatters. They've been giving us a lot of trouble. And the police, well these days they're all . . . they just don't really do anything about it. So we've got to look after ourselves. Us . . . residents.

A pause.

JIMMY   So I'm just warning you.

MTO   Warning me?

JIMMY   About the squatters. And to tell you I'm here if you have any trouble. They often break into places just after someone has moved in. You should get some dogs. Maybe an alarm. And I could weld you a burglar guard for that fan-light. Professional. It's my job. I do burglar guards.

A pause.

MTO   Well, I suppose I should thank you.

JIMMY   What for?

MTO   For looking after my house. My light fittings. My window frames. My kitchen sink.

JIMMY   Oh. Right. You're welcome. And if you ever have trouble, you know who to call.

MTO   Great. I'll remember that.

JIMMY   You should cut the grass too. Long grass makes the place look deserted. They'll think it's a soft target. You often see them walking through the suburb, just looking for opportunities.

MTO   I don't have a lawn-mower.

JIMMY   I've got one. I'll cut the grass for you.

MTO   You don't have to do that. But maybe I can borrow the mower from you some time.

JIMMY   No. No problem. I enjoy it actually. Clears my mind. Some people meditate. Some people pray. I mow. I'll be here Saturday morning.

MTO   I don't want to hassle you.

JIMMY   No hassle. I'll be here.

Jimmy starts walking off. He suddenly stops and turns.

JIMMY   That other post-box.

MTO   The London bus?

JIMMY   Yes. If you're not going to use it, could I buy it off you?

MTO   No.

JIMMY   You want to keep it?

MTO   No, I mean I don't want money. You can have it. For nothing.

JIMMY   No, no, no! No question about it, I must pay. Nothing for nothing. I don't believe in handouts. That's half the problem with this country.

MTO   Tell you what: I give you the post-box, you mow my lawn.

JIMMY   Barter, hey? Well, why not. I suppose this is Africa.

MTO   I suppose it is. See you Saturday.

JIMMY   What time?

MTO   Any time.

JIMMY   African time?

MTO   Sure. African time.

SCENE FOUR

Mto's backyard

Kenneth and Mto are busy improvising their way through a very sketchy synopsis of their idea for the presentation they are preparing for Electric Zebra. They make attempts at sound effects, singing and dancing.

KENNETH   OK. The potential investors are all there in the hushed auditorium. Total darkness. We hear the sounds of night insects.

MTO   Crickets. Maybe a rain-bird in the distance.

KENNETH   OK, OK.

MTO   Or the cry of a fish eagle.

KENNETH   Better. Then we see a faint, orange glow in the dark.

MTO   A glow that silhouettes some figures.

KENNETH   Lighting them from behind. But still too dark to really see what is happening. And then we hear a chant beginning.

MTO   How do you mean a chant?

KENNETH   Just do anything for now. That Juluka song. The one about 'Don't fuck with the lions . . .'

BOTH (*Singing*)   Impi, wo' nans' imp' iyeza, obani bengathinth' amabhubesi.

KENNETH   It's a line of Zulu warriors, spears glinting in the moonlight as they drum the shafts against their shields.

MTO (*Mto stops singing*)   Drum against their shields? Are you sure they did that?

KENNETH   Of course they did.

MTO   How do you know?

KENNETH   I've seen it.

MTO   Where?

KENNETH   That movie. 'Zulu'. Or 'Zulu Dawn'. Michael Caine and ten red-coats versus 10 000 Zulus. Before they go into battle they all drum their shields.

MTO   Why?

KENNETH   I don't know. Because it's scary. Just go with it for now, OK. We can sweat the details later. (*They continue*) The drumming becomes more frenetic and they break out into a full-blooded war-dance. Come on, Mto. Dance. Get with the programme, broer.

MTO (*Mto does a few half-hearted Zulu dance steps*)   And then, out of nowhere, gunshots. They fall, in twos and threes. Dead. The rhythm ends.

KENNETH   I think they could dance for a bit longer before they get shot.

MTO   I thought we were sweating the details later.

KENNETH   Mto, we have to push the dancing. This thing has got to rock them. Rhythm of Africa with four-part harmony.

MTO   No, no, no, no!

KENNETH   What?

MTO   This is for investors, not the Durban beachfront. It's turning into a bloody tourist sideshow. The Coon Carnival.

KENNETH   Investors, tourists, it's all the same. They want happy natives to make them tap their feet.

MTO   Surely we can give them something more sophisticated.

KENNETH   We are. We're building towards our climax: the African Renaissance. A story of triumph over adversity. The rebirth of Africa.

MTO   Oh right, very sophisticated: sad natives who become happy natives.

KENNETH   It's more than that. It's about sad natives and angry natives who then become happy natives.

MTO   And why does it have to be black natives? Why can't it be white natives?

KENNETH   Come on Mto. That's obvious.

MTO   What's obvious? You're the first one to say you're African because you've been here since 1710.

KENNETH   1664.

MTO   Whatever. Are you a native or aren't you?

KENNETH   Yes, but I'm not the sort of native that looks right on a postcard.

MTO   Why not? White Americans have cowboys, white Australians have Crocodile Dundee – why can't you get dressed up as Fanie the Voortrekker?

KENNETH   What!

MTO   I'm being serious.

KENNETH   No way! Crocodile Dundee is a funny guy and cowboys are cool. Us South African whitey's had a useless publicity department.

MTO   So it's OK for a Zulu like me to dress up in fur and feathers that I never wear at any other time, but you won't sit in an ox-wagon because it's uncool?

KENNETH   No, not because it's uncool. Because you wearing fur and feathers looks like a Zulu warrior and me sitting in an ox-wagon with a rifle in my hand would just look like a old racist what used to shoot blacks. The investors will kak!

MTO   How is a Zulu warrior going to help investment?

KENNETH   Because you're all the culture we've got. What is my culture? I come from a French murderer, Scottish cattle thieves, in-bred Dutch farmers and fuck knows what other European 'gommie' leftovers.

MTO   Oh the white man's burden.

KENNETH   I'm serious Mto, you're the Samurai of Africa. The perfect African Renaissance image: a Zulu warrior with the Spear of Knowledge in his hand and the Shield of Truth by his side.

MTO   And the Feathers of Democracy on his head.

KENNETH   You just don't appreciate your . . . Zuluness.

MTO   My Zuluness?

KENNETH   If I was Zulu I'd do the whole thing: get married with cows, goats' blood on the walls, ox blood on the floor, read my bones, speak to my ancestors, the whole trip, broer. Shit, it's even better than being Jewish or Catholic – you have all this stuff you can do that says, 'I'm Zulu'. Roots, Mto

MTO   OK, OK! Go marry a black girl. But forget about the cows – her father's going to want a DVD and a BMW. And if you get any ox-blood on his fancy lounge suite, you'll have to pay the dry-cleaning bills.

The noise of Jimmy's lawn-mower has been getting steadily more intrusive throughout the latter part of his exchange.

KENNETH   Christ that's loud. Who is that guy?

MTO   My neighbour, Jimmy.

KENNETH   He looks like an arsehole. Is that a gun on his belt?

MTO   Ja. Jimmy's a bit of a cowboy. (*To Jimmy*) Sorry Jimmy, what's that? I can't hear you. I said I can't hear you!

The lawn-mower is turned off as Kenneth becomes Jimmy.

JIMMY   I said, you guys are noisy buggers, hey! It's been like a bloody riot all morning. I thought you had a whole tribe there in your backyard.

MTO   Sorry Jimmy. I hope we didn't disturb you.

JIMMY   No. No problem, no problem. I'm just saying. For a moment there I was reaching for my gun. Then I saw it was just you.

MTO   We're rehearsing.

JIMMY   Was that the song about killing farmers? Hey? Isn't that what the words mean? 'Kill the farmers' or 'one settler, one bullet'?

MTO   No, we're just putting something together for a government project.

JIMMY   Oh right. You riding the gravy train? You and your friend here. You must ask them if they've got a ticket for me too, hey! Ask them if the train needs a conductor.

MTO   Actually, the project is about bringing more gravy into the country. It's to encourage investment. Sell South Africa.

JIMMY   Jesus! Well you better change the tune, my friend. You guys toyi-toyi like that they're not gonna be investing, they gonna be on the next plane out of here.

They both react as if Kenneth has just said something.

JIMMY (*To Kenneth*)   You don't have to get cheeky, my boy, it's just a joke.

MTO   Jimmy, this is Kenneth.

JIMMY   Ja well, Kenneth, around here if you're someone's neighbour you get to make a few jokes. Don't know how it is where you live.

MTO   Kenneth has been in working in London, for two years.

JIMMY   Oh right. My old neighbour is living back in London. Maybe you met him there: Terry Rushbrooke. Now there's a guy you could have put in your government concert. He used to do this thing with two cigarettes up his nose and ping pong balls in his cheeks. Those investors would be pissing themselves. One thing about the Pommies, hey: their British humour . . .

MTO   Anyway Jimmy, I suppose I'll see you Saturday, same as usual. Kenneth and I should probably get back to work now.

JIMMY   You theatre types, hey. The world is all a stage, and all the men and boys are playing. You see Kenneth. We're not all savages here in Woodlands. We talk Shakespeare over the fence. Christ, what is that on your eyebrow! You get into a fight? I hope the other guy looks as bad.

MTO   Body piercing.

JIMMY   Shit, what's gonna be next? A bone through the nose? Looks like we're all heading back to the jungle here. Anyway, see you Saturday. Same as usual.

MTO   Same as usual.

Jimmy switches to Kenneth.

KENNETH   You guys in charge of the Woodlands Shakespeare society, or something?

MTO   Jimmy mows my lawn.

KENNETH   A black homeowner with a white gardener.

MTO   Like I said he's a nice guy.

KENNETH   Big gun for a nice guy.

MTO   It's a licensed gun. And he's part of the Neighbourhood Watch.

KENNETH   You don't know these people, Mto. I do. That face. That attitude. I'm telling you, China, there's blood on those hands.

MTO   Oh bullshit Kenneth. If he's such a big racist, then why does he mow my lawn?

KENNETH   He's protecting his investment.

MTO   His investment? What do you mean?

15

KENNETH   Does he mow the grass for his other neighbour?

MTO   No, the other neighbour has his own lawn-mower.

KENNETH   You mean he's also white.

MTO   Why are you so interested in who cuts my grass?

KENNETH   I'm interested in *why* he's cutting your grass.

MTO   Because it's long!

KENNETH   It's damage control, broer. You think white suburbia is lapping you up. Bullshit! A black person moves in, they all start kakking off, nipping straws.

MTO   And what has this got to do with mowing my lawn?

KENNETH   Damage control. When he has to sell, buyers will think, 'Well, the guy next door is black, but he mows the lawn, so he must be one of the good ones.'

A pause.

MTO   Yesterday there's this knock at my door. And I open it, and there's a little white boy standing there. And he says, 'Good afternoon Sir, will you please take a ticket for my school raffle.' So I do. I choose ticket number five because that's the number of my new house. And I give the kid his five rand and he smiles and says, 'Thank you very much, Sir.'

Kenneth shrugs.

MTO   It's the first time any white kid has called me 'Sir'. He just took me in his stride like I'm part of the scenery. For the first time I don't feel like a visitor. Things are happening here in Woodlands that you can't see. Good things. Maybe you're the one with the problem. Would you buy a house next to me?

KENNETH   Actually, no.

MTO   Shit Kenneth, that's a hell of a thing to admit.

KENNETH   I'd live next door to you. Hell, I'd live with you, no problem. But I wouldn't buy a house anywhere in this country. Property sucks. It's a kak investment. A trap, broer. Take the bait and you're gone like a scone.

MTO   You know what? I'm just here to live. Not to buy and sell. This is my house. I grew up walking through white suburbs like this one. And I never dreamt that one day I would live here. And I really like it here. If the people here like keeping their grass short, well then, I'm going to keep mine short as well.

KENNETH   Fuck it, broer. Your grass roots are showing. What's this now, you mowing for freedom?

MTO   Look, it's lunchtime. Why don't I go fetch us a bunny chow from the corner shop?

KENNETH   Ja, good idea.

MTO   You coming?

KENNETH   No. I'm going to stay and work on a few bits.

MTO   Mutton or chicken?

KENNETH   You choose. But make sure he adds lots of gravy. Like Jimmy says, this is the gravy train.

SCENE FIVE

Patel's Corner Shop

The interior of a take-away/general dealer. Patel is behind the counter and Mto is browsing. Patel is shouting at a teenager who is playing video games.

PATEL   Hey, lightie! Ja you. You don't come into my shop and hit my machines. How you behave at home? You hit your father's video machine? Ja well, you don't hit my games machine. Right? (*To imaginary customer*) These children today, whatever colour they are, they got no respect, man. When I was that age, I was working in this shop. Fifteen years old. Mr Anastasos, the Greek, he was the owner then. Now 45 years since I started sweeping this floor, I'm the owner. Everyone always ask me, 'Hey Patel, you Indian, man! Why you don't call your shop The Curry Den or Patel's Roadhouse? Why you call it The Olympus Café and Takeaway?' And I tell them, respect – because I got a respect for Mr Anastasos. Me, I'm also respectable. So, why these lighties give me no respect? (*To another customer*) What you want? What you want? (*Shouting to the kitchen behind him*) Give me one Frank, two Russians, one Dagwood burger and three packet chips. (*To Mto who is browsing around the shelves*) Hey! Wena! Hayi thinta lo mpashla ka mina. Nokho wena funa thenga lo into wena buyisa lapha wena thenga, kodwa hayi thintha, thintha, thintha because wena zo ngcolisa manje zonke impashla ka mina and then mina hayi azi dayisa lo mpashla. Please! Hayi thintha, thintha, thintha.

MTO   Actually, I'm buying this.

PATEL   Oh. You speak English.

MTO   Yes. I was looking for some ant poison.

PATEL   There it is. Top shelf. Anything else?

MTO   Give me a chicken curry bunny chow.

PATEL   Half? Quarter? What size you want?

MTO   Half.

PATEL (*Shouting to the kitchen*)   Give me one half chicken bunny!

MTO   Lots of gravy.

PATEL   Extra gravy!

A pause.

PATEL   You from the squatter camp?

MTO   No, no! I stay up the road. Been here a few weeks.

PATEL   You know those fellows are breaking in all the time, everywhere. They always stealing from me as well. Shoplifting. That's why I got a security guard here, full time. Costs me leg and a foot, man. But what can you do – they'll kill you for a loaf of bread.

MTO   You should get a gun. Like my neighbour.

PATEL   No, man. Mr Du Plessis, in the hardware store they killed him with his own gun. Overpowered him, you know. I stood there when he died. Half an hour we waited – no police, no ambulance. Blood everywhere. Every day I wake up and think, maybe today they'll get me too. That's why I was treating you suspicious just now, you know, because I was thinking you one of the squatters. It's hard to tell. But, now I know you own a house, so that's different. Where you were before?

MTO   Umlazi township.

PATEL   Oh, so you upgrading. I own a shop in the white area. That's one thing. But to buy a house, I'm not so sure.

MTO   Why not?

PATEL   White is white. Am I right? Like these lighties with no respect. Whose house you bought?

MTO   Terry Rushbrooke.

PATEL   Oh, Mr Rushbrooke. I knew him well, many years. English fellow, you know, from England, there by Britain.

MTO   Yes, I know where England is. I've been there myself, actually.

PATEL   Mr Rushbrooke used to say, 'You don't use rabbit meat, so why you call it a bunny chow?' And I would tell him, 'Hell, Mr Rushbrooke, if you not from Durban then how I can explain it? It's just a Durban thing.' And he would say, 'It's not a Durban thing; it's bread from Britain and curry from India. That's not a bunny chow, it's a curry sandwich.'

MTO   Sounds like an idiot.

PATEL   No man, a real joker, make you laugh like you going to die. One time Mr Rushbrooke took a lid from a dustbin, and a broom stick and he was dancing just like a Zulu warrior. Kicking his legs right up. Hell, funny man. So quiet now without him. Terrible business, you know.

MTO   What was?

PATEL   Terrible tragedy, man. You know Mr Louw, your neighbour.

MTO   Jimmy Louw. Yes?

PATEL   His wife was murdered, man. Right there in the house. Cold blood.

MTO   By Mr Rushbrooke?

PATEL   No man! The squatters. Shot her. With her own gun. Just like Mr Du Plessis. And Mr Rushbrooke, he said he can't live in a place like that, so he's going back home. Oh, there you go, your food is ready: one half chicken bunny. (*To another customer*) Ja, ja, what you want, what you want?

SCENE SIX

Mto's backyard

Kenneth is working on a part of the presentation. Prudence appears at the fence singing.

PRUDENCE   Hello master.

KENNETH   Hey?

PRUDENCE   I said, hello master. I am Prudence. I am the girl for next door. I am working for Master Jimmy. I was being on holiday and now I am back and I am too much happy we are having a new neighbour. So I am saying: 'hello master'.

KENNETH   Sawubona, Prudence.

PRUDENCE   Sorry?

KENNETH   I said 'sawubona'. Hello.

PRUDENCE   Oh, sawubona. I am the girl, the cleaning girl for Master Jimmy. I was used to be his nanny when he was little boy, even for changing the nappies when I was working for the mother and the father for Master Jimmy. Now I am the girl for cooking and for cleaning. That is me master: Prudence.

KENNETH   Don't call me master. I am Kenneth.

PRUDENCE   Kenneth? What is Kenneth?

KENNETH   Me. My name is Kenneth.

PRUDENCE   Oh, you are Master Kenneth!

KENNETH   No, just Kenneth.

PRUDENCE   My English, she is bad. What is 'just Kenneth'?

KENNETH   Never mind. Hello Prudence. Nice to meet you.

PRUDENCE   Master Kenneth, are you having children?

KENNETH   No, I'm not ready for children.

PRUDENCE   Hawu shame! You are not having a wife.

KENNETH   No. I've got no money for cows. For lobola.

PRUDENCE   For lobola. (*She laughs*) There is no one for doing your cleaning.

KENNETH   No Prudence, I do my own cleaning and ironing.

PRUDENCE   Hawu, you are ironing and cleaning. So much work. Hawu shame, you are not having a nanny.

KENNETH   No nanny, no kids, no woman, no cry.

PRUDENCE   Master Kenneth, you are sick.

KENNETH   What?

PRUDENCE   Hawu, Nkosi yami! Your eye, it is sick?

KENNETH   Oh, no, no. It's for jewellery. Like an earring.

PRUDENCE   Oh.

A pause.

PRUDENCE   Master Kenneth I am having a small problem. I was used to have a garden there in the bushes behind all the houses. I was used to plant pumpkin and mealie and monkey nut. But now the squatters they came and they break everything. They take all my vegetables and they leave nothing. Now I am too scared to go there because the squatters they are too much bad people.

KENNETH   They are just hungry, Prudence.

PRUDENCE   Sorry?

KENNETH   They are hungry. The squatters. They just want food.

PRUDENCE   Yes master, they just want to steal all my food. Now I am praying to God to look after my vegetables, but I think God she's very busy because there is so much troubles and God she does not have the time for to look after my vegetables also. So I am asking for you that I can make a small garden there by the back by this house?

KENNETH   It's not up to me.

PRUDENCE   Master Jimmy, she's not wanting any garden to his house. She's only wanting short grass with the lawn-mower. She's not wanting any flower or pumpkin. So I am asking for you that I can plant a small garden at the back by your house and then I will give you some pumpkin and some mielie and some monkey nut.

KENNETH   It's not my house.

PRUDENCE   Yes, behind your house. At the back. A small garden.

KENNETH   No, I said it is not my house. You must ask Mto.

PRUDENCE   Mto? Who is Mto? He is your garden boy?

KENNETH   Mto is the man who bought this house. It is his house. You must ask him when he gets back from the shop.

PRUDENCE   Hawu bakithi! There is a Zulu boy living to this house?

KENNETH   Yes, he is Zulu.

PRUDENCE   Hawu! A Zulu boy bought Mr Rushbrooke's house?

KENNETH   A Zulu man, yes.

PRUDENCE   A Zulu man.

KENNETH   Look there he is, he's coming back now. You must ask him about the garden. Mto, this is Prudence.

PRUDENCE (*Talking to Mto*)   Yebo, sawubona mfana. I am staying next door. I am working for Master Jimmy. Ngeke Mfana. I am never speak Zulu when there is a white man. It is not polite for Master Kenneth.

KENNETH   She called me Master Kenneth, OK. Prudence, my name is Kenneth, and you can talk Zulu in front of me, it's fine.

PRUDENCE   Hayi, hayi, hayi, hayi, hayi! The parents for Master Jimmy were always telling me, Prudence, when we are here you must talk only English. Uyabona mfana, you can't come in the white houses here and speak Zulu everywhere. You must speak English, then everyone is happy.

Prudence becomes Mto.

KENNETH   Prudence wants to ask you something.

MTO   Ufunani Ma? Ngithi ufunani? Cha, ayikho inkinga. We can speak Zulu here, this is my house. Ungakhuluma. KwaMagaye la. KwaNdosi.

KENNETH   What she's trying to ask you is whether she can plant a vegetable garden in your yard. I think it'll be cool, she'll give you mielies, pumpkins, hey Prudence . . .

MTO *(To Kenneth)*   Hey! I'm the Zulu here, OK. I don't need you to translate. *(To Prudence)* Ya Ma. Usho ukuthini mawuthi ufun' ukutshala?

KENNETH   Tell him Prudence, it's fine . . .

MTO   Kenneth, will you just shut up?

Mto becomes Prudence.

PRUDENCE   Hayi, hayi Master Kenneth, is OK. I find another garden. *(To Mto)* Cha mfana, angifun' ukunihlupa. I don't like to make troubles for Master Kenneth. I find another garden.

Prudence becomes Mto. A pause as Mto and Kenneth watch her go.

KENNETH   You need to lighten up, broer.

MTO   I think you should stay out of this 'Master' Kenneth.

KENNETH   What's the problem? I think it's cool. Organic vegetables in your own backyard.

MTO   I buy my vegetables Kenneth, this is the twenty-first century. We're not still peasants.

KENNETH   And then get a few goats and chickens as well. Maybe a cow, hey. That'll get them running for their passports just like the Pommy who was here before you.

MTO   I have to live here, OK.

KENNETH   Oh, I get it. You're scared of the fascist arsehole with the gun.

MTO   I'm not scared of him.

KENNETH   He's a bloody control freak.

MTO   The guy has had a shit time, OK. The squatters broke into his house. They murdered his wife.

KENNETH   Really? Well, he's got bad karma. What goes around comes around.

MTO   That's a shit thing to say. And tell me, is it just because I'm black you think I should let some old black woman I don't even know turn my yard into a farm?

Mto's cell phone rings. Kenneth becomes Chenaye on her phone.

MTO   Ko Ko. Come in.

CHENAYE   Mto?

MTO   Yes.

CHENAYE   Hello howzit. It's Chenaye, Chenaye de Villiers. From Electric Zebra.

MTO   Oh, right. Hello.

CHENAYE   Sawubona.

MTO   Sorry.

CHENAYE   I said 'Sawubona'. I'm learning Zulu. Did I say it wrong?

MTO   Oh. No, that was fine. Sawubona.

CHENAYE   Unjani wena ngisaphila.

MTO   OK, you got the question right there.

CHENAYE   I did? Oh good.

MTO   But then you answered it yourself.

CHENAYE   Oh damn. Well I guess you'll just have to teach me when I see you.

MTO   Oh. Are you coming down to Durban?

CHENAYE   Yes. And I was wondering if you were free for lunch next Wednesday.

MTO   Lunch?

CHENAYE   Just to discuss a few things. Over a bottle of wine perhaps. Just us two. I'm thinking you and I need to talk one on one about our relationship.

MTO   Our relationship?

CHENAYE   Look, we hardly know each other, that's what you're thinking isn't it?

MTO   Oh, no, no, no. You're right. We should meet.

CHENAYE   Yes I think we should. I can just sense that there is a potential chemistry here.

MTO   Do you think so?

CHENAYE   Absolutely. Lunch on me, Wednesday. Sala kahle.

MTO   Ja. You too. Uphile.

Chenaye becomes Kenneth.

MTO   So, let's go and have some bunny chow. It's in the kitchen.

KENNETH   Who was that?

MTO   Just Chenaye.

KENNETH   Oh, just Chenaye?

MTO   Ja.

KENNETH   What did she want?

MTO   Just chatting.

KENNETH   A social call?

MTO   Ja, more or less.

KENNETH   More or less. What does that mean?

MTO   She just happens to be passing through Durban next week and she wants to take me out to lunch.

KENNETH   Oh, right.

MTO   What?

KENNETH   Two's company, hey? I'm not invited?

MTO   She knows you already. She obviously wants to talk to me a bit more and make sure I'm right for the project.

KENNETH   Oh, I think she's pretty sure you're right. You're right like dynamite, broer. I just don't think it's this project she has in mind.

MTO   Bullshit!

KENNETH   It's cool, go ahead, dip your wick. Try some vanilla. Just don't get attached, China, or you're cruising for a bruising.

MTO   A bruising? Because she likes me?

KENNETH   I didn't say that. She just wants to see if all the stories are true. I'm sure you won't disappoint.

MTO   You're talking such shit. I'm hungry.

KENNETH   Well, then let's eat. We need to start building your stamina for your lunch.

MTO   Piss off Kenneth.

SCENE SEVEN

Mto's and Jimmy's backyards

Mto is clearing junk from his garage. Jimmy is making burglar guards. An angle-grinder is heard screaming and then winding down as it turns off.

JIMMY   You very quiet today. Your concert finished?

MTO   No. Kenneth's at the doctor. His eye. So, shouldn't you wear ear-plugs when you use that thing?

JIMMY   Oh. Did I wake you up?

MTO No, been in the garage all day. It's full of shit. So I'm throwing most of it away.

JIMMY How can you just throw it away? It's been there for years.

MTO That's the point. Most of it is rusted, or broken or just useless.

JIMMY But it's Terry's stuff.

MTO It was Terry's stuff? I got it with the house, and I want it out. I'm leaving it all on the pavement, so you can help yourself if you want to scratch through it.

JIMMY Hey, you can't throw those away. Terry's magic wands.

MTO Magic wands?

JIMMY Ja, Terry Rushbrooke was a magician. You know, someone who does magic, like a witch-doctor.

MTO I know what a magician is, I just hadn't seen a wand before.

JIMMY He did magic tricks for children's parties. He was a showman, like you. Hell man, old Terry was a funny oke. Funniest oke I've ever known.

MTO Yes, I've heard all about it. His Zulu warrior act. With the broom and the dustbin lid.

JIMMY Oh, that. That was nothing compared to his other stuff.

MTO You mean it gets funnier?

JIMMY Ja man. You had to be sharp around old Terry. He had the gift of the gab, man. Just the way he said things. The life and soul of every party. Wish he was still around.

MTO And now you have to make do with me as your neighbour.

JIMMY Didn't mean it like that. But he was like ten people, old Terry. Had his own mobile disco for parties. And he was the Father Christmas every year at the bowling club.

MTO I was also Father Christmas once.

JIMMY Bullshit! You serious?

MTO   Ja, it was my first acting job, seventeen years old. I had to stand outside Commercial Furnishers in West Street, dressed as Father Christmas.

JIMMY   And what did you have to do?

MTO   Ngenani, ngenani! Sidayisa izihlalo namatafula. (*Mto gives a deliberately over-the-top performance of a street salesman trying to encourage passers-by to enter a shop. He ends on a big:*) Happy, happy Christmas!

JIMMY   That's Africa for you, hey. Everything backward.

MTO   Backward?

JIMMY   No I mean like . . . for all of us. Take Christmas Day. You know – ham, turkey, roast mutton, roast potatoes – and it's hot enough outside to fry an egg on the pavement. Eating like eskimoes, sweating like pigs. Backward.

MTO   You mean back to front.

JIMMY   Same difference.

MTO   I've never really had Christmas like that. Not the way you guys do, with the turkey and everything.

JIMMY   You need tradition. It keeps you on the rails, like going to church. Old Terry used to always say that's the one thing he missed most about not being home at Christmas. The cold. He always called England home.

MTO   Oh. Well, he's got what he wanted then. He's back home now, he doesn't have to make do with fake snow or a black Santa Claus. As a kid, I was terrified when I heard about this white man with a big beard who breaks into your house. I thought he was like the police, or the army.

JIMMY   What do mean, 'breaks into your house'? The cops, the army, they didn't break in. They were searching. Following orders.

MTO   Call it what you like. They were scary, back in the eighties, coming into our house in the middle of the night.

JIMMY   Why did the cops search your house?

MTO My father was an activist.

JIMMY An activist?

MTO Ja. In the ANC.

JIMMY Like a terrorist? I mean . . . insurgent?

MTO Guerrilla? Ja . . . sort of. Anyway, when I heard about this big, fat white man coming into your house, I was glad we didn't have Christmas like the white kids.

JIMMY I think you had him confused with that little Zulu thing that comes to get you when you're sleeping. What do you call it?

MTO Tokoloshe.

JIMMY Ja. So do you guys really believe that stuff?

MTO No man! It's just like you guys and Father Christmas.

JIMMY Then why does Prudence put her bed up on bricks so that the tokoloshe can't reach her when she's sleeping?

MTO Ask her. I'm not Prudence, OK. I'm just the same colour, that's all.

JIMMY Oh ja? Then why do you slaughter goats whenever I go away?

MTO I don't slaughter goats.

JIMMY Yes you do. Behind my back.

MTO I slaughtered one goat. Openly, in broad daylight, in my backyard. And if you'd been here, it would have made no difference.

JIMMY But why? This is the suburbs. If you want a braai why can't you buy your meat from the coolie shop like everyone else?

MTO It wasn't a braai. It was to welcome my father to my new house.

JIMMY He's moving in?

MTO His spirit. He wasn't allowed to live here when he was alive. So I think it's right he should be here now – even if you can't see him.

JIMMY Is this also like Father Christmas?

MTO No. Like you said: it's tradition – keeps you on the rails.

JIMMY   Anyway, Father Christmas is actually the opposite of a thief. He breaks in, but then he gives instead of takes.

MTO   Well, in South Africa it would still be breaking and entering, because there's no chimney to climb down.

JIMMY   Ja, I suppose if we did have chimneys here it would just be one more way for these bastards to get into our houses. The squatters, I mean.

A pause.

MTO   Sorry to hear about your wife.

JIMMY   Ja. It's alright.

MTO   I hear that's why Terry left.

JIMMY   Says who?

MTO   Patel. Mr Patel from the corner shop.

JIMMY   That old coolie must mind his own business. Indians, always sticking their noses in where they don't belong.

MTO   Sorry, I didn't mean to . . .

JIMMY   No, no, no, it's fine. I'm just saying. Old Patel, whatever he says you divide by four. You know how it is with Indians. Terry went back to look after his sick mother. Poor bastard, sixty years old and he's back with his mom.

A pause.

JIMMY   So, your father, was he in jail?

MTO   He was detained for a bit. But then he left the country. For training.

JIMMY   Like a soldier, you mean.

MTO   Yes.

JIMMY   Did he fight in Angola?

MTO   Maybe.

JIMMY   You must know.

MTO   Didn't see him again.

JIMMY   And you heard nothing?

MTO   We heard he was killed.

JIMMY   Anyway, like they say, it's history now.

MTO   Ja. Water under the bridge.

JIMMY   Do your grass Saturday, same as usual? Hey?

MTO   Oh, ja. Can't let the grass grow, better keep it neat.

JIMMY   Old Prudence hasn't given you any of her nonsense has she?

MTO   What kind of nonsense?

JIMMY   You know Prudence. She's a bit . . .

MTO   Backward.

JIMMY   Well, back to front. You can buy vegetables for bugger all from the coolie shop down the road, but she still wants to cover my yard in pumpkins.

MTO   Don't worry, nobody tells me what to do.

JIMMY   Glad to hear it.

SCENE EIGHT

A restaurant

Chenaye and Mto are sitting at a table.

CHENAYE   Glad you could make it.

MTO   Well, I'm glad to be here.

CHENAYE   Mina ngiyajabula ukuvakasha eThekwini.

MTO   That's great. The Zulu's coming along.

CHENAYE   Well, I feel it's our duty as white South Africans. Look how many black people speak English. If we are going to be part of Africa, we must all speak an African language, don't you think?

MTO   Absolutely. I'm impressed.

CHENAYE   It helps as well with my black clients. Opens doors like that. Gee, it's so good to be back in the first world. Well, I think Durban still qualifies as first world?

MTO   Just. But we're working on it.

CHENAYE   Sorry?

MTO   Where've you been?

CHENAYE   Had a business meeting in Zimbabwe. All for nothing – the client has pulled out. Cold feet. It was going to be a major tourist development. So sad. So sad. A great treasure like the Victoria Falls, and the place is dying.

MTO   Well, like they say: you can't choose your neighbours.

CHENAYE   Too true. And you know, whenever I go to Zim I have to leave my gun behind.

MTO   You have a gun?

CHENAYE   God yes! These days I feel naked without it. Especially up there. I just hope this place doesn't go the same way. They could drag us down with them, you know. They've just got to get their house in order.

MTO   Ja. They must mow their lawn, hey. Keep the grass neat.

CHENAYE   Oh, listen to you. You're such a scream. People say the black sense of humour is different, but it's just the same, isn't it.

MTO   What was the flight like?

CHENAYE   Awful. Had to fly here from Harare. And would you believe it, business class was full. Had to sit all squashed up in economy. Don't you hate it when that happens?

MTO   Oh. Yes. Economy. Hate it.

CHENAYE   Of course, it depends who you're squashed up with.

MTO   Yes.

CHENAYE   But we make do. It's just part of being South African, dropping your standards.

MTO   So, you said I shouldn't bring Kenneth along. Why?

CHENAYE   Well, there are things you and I need to talk about. I'm not quite sure how to put it.

MTO   Well, just say it. I can take it, I'm a big boy.

CHENAYE   Kenneth's out.

MTO   What?

CHENAYE   Kenneth is out.

MTO   Sorry, I don't know . . .

CHENAYE   Out of the project. What else would I be talking about?

MTO   Of course. Sorry . . . But, we've been working for weeks, I don't understand.

CHENAYE   I've decided to use the pitch to sell your talents to the client. Kenneth will be paid for what he's done so far. That's business. Mto, let me level with you. You have a rare talent. And I have a great sense of vision for that talent.

MTO   How do you mean?

CHENAYE   I mean money, Mto. Your place is in the corporate world.

MTO   I'm an artist Chenaye.

CHENAYE   So, you're saying money's not important?

MTO   Well, I wouldn't say not important . . .

CHENAYE   How much money have you made from the play about your father? Or should I say, 'how much money have you lost?'

MTO   That's not the point . . .

CHENAYE   No, the point is: South Africans have had the truth commission, Mto, they don't want it on stage any more. Even the Germans are losing interest in African suffering. And let's face it, if every victim claims to be a hero, well then we're all heroes, aren't we?

MTO   I don't have to listen to this . . .

CHENAYE   Hear me out! Your play is great, but guilt doesn't have a market any more, Mto, good products do. And you are good. Your face, your ability, my contacts, my money – we could do anything from rebranding old, white products for a new black market; to setting you up as a black Dale Carnegie. I can show you the figures you'll be earning.

MTO   I feel a bit bad about Kenneth . . .

CHENAYE   Look, Mto, you have affirmative action written all over your face. Kenneth knows he could never get work like this without you as a front-man.

MTO   But he lined this project up for me.

CHENAYE   Yes, but it's getting tricky. It's a government project with a government official. Also Zulu. A Mr Xaba (*She mispronounces it*).

MTO   Xaba.

CHENAYE   Yes. And . . . how do I put this . . . if there are too many white faces involved, we're not going to get the contract. It's already been a bit of a struggle dealing with him on my own. And Kenneth can rub people up the wrong way. I've told Mr Xaba (*She still mispronounces Xaba*) Kenneth's input is only for the initial stages. I need to know that you're going to stay on board. I can assure you, my cheques don't bounce.

A pause.

MTO   Look, I don't like it. I need to think about this.

CHENAYE   Kenneth is out either way. So don't feel responsible for that.

MTO   You know what Kenneth thinks? He thinks this lunch is a pick up. That you're after me.

CHENAYE   Oh my God, that's hysterical. He thinks I want you and me to . . . That's ridiculous.

MTO   That's what I thought.

CHENAYE   Not that I wouldn't, I mean . . . I love black men. Samuel L. Jackson, what's not to love?

MTO   Should I do an American accent?

CHENAYE You use any accent you want – just as long as you say 'yes'.

A pause.

MTO Looks like you need me more than I need you.

CHENAYE I don't ask twice, Mto. And I think we both know you're in no position to turn this down.

MTO Shall we eat.

CHENAYE What about the sole? I believe it's divine here. But then I know about you guys and seafood. My maid, lovely woman, like a mother to me, she once told me that to a Zulu eating prawns is like eating cockroaches.

MTO Well, we're not all peasants. Look at Samuel L. Jackson.

CHENAYE No, man. I mean it's like a cultural thing, isn't it? Not eating seafood.

MTO (*To the waiter*) I'll have the prawn curry.

CHENAYE Make that two! You eat prawns?

MTO Well, I eat curry. And I'll try anything once.

CHENAYE I can't wait to tell Florence. My maid. She just won't believe me.

MTO Tell her I also have a very neat lawn and a white gardener. That'll really surprise her.

CHENAYE You're joking.

MTO I'm not. And my white gardener carries a gun, so he doubles as a security guard.

CHENAYE Now that's one of the great things about the New South Africa. At last white people are accepting that menial jobs are not just for black people.

MTO Tell me. Your maid, Florence?

CHENAYE Yes.

MTO   Does she plant anything in your garden?

CHENAYE   Ooh no, I get a gardening service in. Florence doesn't know the first thing about gardening.

MTO   No, I mean, do you let her grow pumpkins and mielies?

CHENAYE   God no! She wanted to, but I'm landscaped. Cost me a fortune, I can't throw that investment away with pumpkins growing all over the place. I said, 'Florence, you don't need to grow vegetables, I'll buy them for you from Woolworths'. Anyway, I think it's against the by-laws. My neighbours are very conservative. They'd blow a fuse if I let my maid start farming.

MTO   I think it's time we said fuck the by-laws, don't you? Remind neighbours like yours that we live in Africa.

CHENAYE (*To the waiter*)   Actually, I've changed my mind. Do you still do that wonderful sushi platter? I'll have that. (*To Mto*) You won't believe this, but the Sushi chef here, he's black. Zulu, in fact.

MTO   Really.

CHENAYE   Yes. He started off as a dishwasher. Isn't that amazing? I read an article about him. Apparently his family thinks he's mad and none of them will touch sushi. But he virtually lives on it. Raw fish! A Zulu sushi chef. What next?

MTO   A Zulu Samurai.

CHENAYE   I wouldn't be surprised. It's a crazy country this. You have to just love it.

MTO   Yes. Guns, lawn-mowers and fish-eating Zulus. What more could anyone want?

SCENE NINE

Mto's backyard

Kenneth is busy trying to perfect a part of a dance routine. Prudence is in the background – gardening. She sings to herself. A Zulu Christian hymn.

Kenneth stops, exasperated because he can't get the steps right. He starts rolling a joint.

KENNETH   Hi there, Prudence.

PRUDENCE   Hello Master Kenneth.

KENNETH   Garden's growing nicely.

PRUDENCE   Yes, Master Kenneth, she's growing nicely now.

KENNETH   Are those mielies? You're going to make some mielie-bread for us one day. Some Jeqe.

PRUDENCE (*Laughing*)   Hawu, Master Kenneth, you know Jeqe.

KENNETH   Yes, Prudence. I'm a whitey, but I'm an African whitey.

PRUDENCE   What is a whitey, Master Kenneth?

KENNETH   No, I'm just saying I'm white . . .

PRUDENCE   Yes, you are white.

KENNETH   But I speak some Zulu.

PRUDENCE   Oh, you speak Zulu. Uyasazi isiZulu? Uthanda ukudla ujeqe njeng' omunt' omnyama?

KENNETH   Well, I speak a little bit of Zulu. But you lost me there.

PRUDENCE   Oh, Master Kenneth, you speak a little bit. Like my English.

KENNETH   No, your English is good. Very good.

PRUDENCE   Oh thank you Master Kenneth.

KENNETH   So, tell me Prudence, what is your real Zulu name?

PRUDENCE   No master, my name is Prudence.

KENNETH   But you must have a Zulu name, like Mto.

PRUDENCE   Oh. (*A pause*) My Zulu name is not good. It is Lahliwe.

KENNETH   Lahliwe?

PRUDENCE   You know Lahliwe?

KENNETH No, what does it mean?

PRUDENCE It means 'thrown away'. Because my father was a bad man who would not look after my mother, so my mother she said I 'throw away'.

KENNETH But you must be proud of your name. It is your Zulu name.

PRUDENCE No master, it is not a nice name.

KENNETH I will call you Lahliwe. You shouldn't call yourself Prudence. Lahliwe sounds cool.

Kenneth gets up to practise some dance steps.

KENNETH Not bad for a whitey, hey Lahliwe?

Prudence laughs.

KENNETH I am not Kenneth any more.

PRUDENCE You are not Kenneth?

KENNETH No, I am Izinyawoziyaduma.

PRUDENCE (*Laughing*) Izinyawoziyaduma.

KENNETH Now we both have two names. You are Prudence Lahliwe and I am Kenneth Izinyawoziyaduma.

PRUDENCE Hawu Bandla, you have a nice Zulu name Master Kenneth. You are dancing like a Zulu boy.

Kenneth dances again. Prudence becomes Mto, watching.

KENNETH Hey broer, check this.

He dances.

KENNETH I'm not Kenneth any more, I'm Izinyawoziyaduma. Ask Lahliwe.

MTO You're not fucking feet of thunder. You're head full of smoke. Ikhandalinentuthu. You talk such crap when you smoke that shit. And we've still got work to do. (*Mto snatches the joint from Kenneth and throws it away. To Prudence:*) Sorry Ma.

KENNETH   Chill broer, it's all under control.

MTO   No, we've got to get this right Kenneth, the presentation is tomorrow. This government guy is going to be there. Mr Xaba.

KENNETH   How do you know that?

MTO   Didn't you tell me?

KENNETH   No.

MTO   Maybe it was Chenaye.

KENNETH   What else did she tell you?

MTO   I wasn't listening. I told you, she was all over me.

KENNETH   So then, what's the problem?

MTO   We need to keep this professional. Be prepared for anything.

KENNETH   Look, this stuffed suit is going to be some useless affirmative action appointee who doesn't have a clue what he wants anyway. He'll take whatever we throw at him.

MTO   How can you say that?

KENNETH   Because he's in government. All the good affirmative action candidates have got real jobs.

The sound of a police van screeching to a halt.

MTO   What the hell is this?

KENNETH   Shit.

MTO   Fuck it, Kenneth! I've told you not smoke here. Go wait inside! I'll deal with this.

Kenneth disappears to become the policeman.

MTO   Hello.

COP (*Looking at Mto suspiciously*)   Wena sebenza lapha?

MTO   Yes.

COP   Lo baas. Biza lo baas ka wena.

MTO   Sorry?

COP   Your baas. Call your baas. I saw him go into the house.

MTO   My baas? Oh. I'm the baas.

COP   Hey?

MTO   This is my house.

COP   Then why did you tell me you worked here?

MTO   I do. I am . . . Look, can I help you?

COP   What are all these weapons lying around here? Spears. Shit, that's an AK47! What are you doing with an assault rifle?

MTO   It's not real. It's for a show.

COP   A show? Why are you doing a show with AK47's?

MTO   It's a government project. How can I help you?

COP   We received a complaint that someone was seen waving weapons around in this yard and making some very suspicious noises.

MTO   The show is a bit noisy. We dance and sing.

COP   Dance and sing?

MTO   Yes. Is that a crime?

COP   We received a complaint and I had to investigate. Maybe just keep the noise down and don't wave those things around so much. Sometimes old Jimmy overreacts a bit. We don't want to get him all worked up.

MTO   Jimmy? Did Jimmy call you out here?

COP   Ja.

MTO   What is his problem?

COP   Look, don't take it personal. He hasn't been right since his wife's . . . accident.

MTO   You call that an accident?

COP   Well, accident, murder, who knows these days . . .

MTO   I can't believe what I'm hearing. No wonder Jimmy 'hasn't been right'. His wife gets murdered and you go around calling it an accident instead of doing your job.

COP   I am doing my job. Jesus, I've been running myself ragged all day. We have one van that's working, we're understaffed, I've had four break-ins, two assaults, a shooting and a dead body this morning alone. And you tell me I'm not doing my job. What do you think this is, a social visit?

MTO   All I know is: you're here giving me uphill about a little bit of noise, and the people who murdered Jimmy's wife are still out there.

COP   Nobody murdered Jimmy's wife. Her gun went off in her handbag. By accident.

MTO   No man! There was a break-in.

COP   No break-in. Nothing taken. It was open and shut: an accident. Even the gun was still there, in her handbag. No thieving bastard is going to leave a gun behind. Not in this country. Jimmy feels guilty, OK. He used to force her to keep a gun. It's a sore point with him. I shouldn't even be telling you this. Now look, let's just keep the peace. I'm going to tell Jimmy you said you'd keep it down. OK?

MTO   Tell him whatever you like.

SCENE TEN

A conference room in a hotel

Mto and Kenneth are about to present the pitch to Chenaye and Mr Xaba, the government official. Kenneth is obviously late and Mto is looking worried. Kenneth then strolls in unaware of Mto's concern.

KENNETH   OK, ready? Can we start? Let's go.

They start performing the pitch. It is a tacky bit of corporate propaganda with flashes of invention and finesse. They are suggesting a piece which is to be performed by a larger cast, so they fill in details with narration as they go.

KENNETH   Watering hole!

MTO   Sunset!

They become animals at a watering hole, using 'physical theatre'.

KENNETH   We see a faint orange glow in the dark.

MTO   A glow that silhouettes some figures, lighting them from behind.

KENNETH   And then we hear a chant beginning.

They 'assume' human form again.

MTO   Babengaphi?

BOTH   Babengapha! Thina singapha! Waf' umuntu!

MTO   Babengaphi?

BOTH   Babengapha! Thina singapha! Waf' umuntu!

They go into a short section of a Zulu war-dance, including the following narration as they dance:

MTO   It's a line of Zulu warriors, spears glinting in the moonlight.

KENNETH   As they drum the shafts against their shields.

MTO   And then, out of nowhere, gunshots.

Mto starts singing a Zulu lament.

KENNETH   We see an old Zulu woman, singing a lament as she makes her way through the bodies of the fallen warriors.

Mto continues singing.

KENNETH   And then, from out of the mist, figures begin to rise. Now they are workers, dressed in overalls and gumboots.

MTO   One of them starts a rhythm that the others pick up on.

They both do a short gumboot dance.

MTO   Industrial warriors, fighting apartheid.

They then go into the following song and end it with the mimed action of throwing a petrol bomb.

BOTH   Sekudala! Kudala sisebenzel' amabhunu. We basebenzi! Basebenzi mas'hlangane.

MTO   Africa. Battle ground where the blood of Africa's children for centuries fed only the tree of sorrow. Where the only harvest was the bitter fruit of hate.

KENNETH   But now, in the new millennium.

MTO   A new dawn. The African Renaissance.

KENNETH   The African Samurai. The new Zulu warriors here for the dawn of the African century.

MTO   Businessmen. Armed with laptops.

The presentation ends and Mto and Kenneth address Chenaye and Xaba, their 'audience'.

MTO   Then the lights would probably fade.

KENNETH   Obviously there would be a cast of around ten.

MTO   It loses something with just the two of us, Baba Xaba. This is just to give you an idea.

KENNETH   But Mto would lead the group.

MTO   And we'd probably do the narration as a voice-over.

KENNETH   And, depending on budget, there are pyrotechnics, video projections. If you want to really make an impact we can go multi-media in a big way.

Kenneth and Mto switch to being Chenaye and Xaba.

XABA   Miss De Villiers?

Chenaye indicates Xaba should respond first.

XABA   OK. I am not categorically sure in fact whether actually you are show-casing our country to best advantage with the approach you have chosen to the task at hand.

CHENAYE   I think the point Mr Xaba is trying to make is that the government is going to be investing a lot of money in this project and we need to be on line with our message.

XABA   You have used the African Renaissance as a focal point as such. That is something most definitely that we in government consider to be very important as a priority.

CHENAYE   Crucial.

XABA   But I am wondering at this particular point in time, whether the African Renaissance is something that the people at large can see.

CHENAYE   People are visual. Very visual. I'm with you, I'm with you.

XABA   What we're talking about here in fact is not an intangible concept as such. We are packaging so to speak a country. Finding that essence that is, by and large: South Africa.

CHENAYE   Exactly, that quintessential something.

XABA   Taking that essence and distilling it . . .

CHENAYE   Distilling.

XABA   Into a first grade product . . .

CHENAYE   Export quality.

XABA   So that South Africa becomes a brand name . . .

CHENAYE   A logo.

XABA   As familiar to the world as The Lion King.

CHENAYE   Something infectious, catchy, that will spread around the globe.

XABA   Not AIDS of course . . . Now, if we select you for the project, you will obviously be allowed total creative freedom . . .

CHENAYE   Within the bounds of the brief.

XABA   . . . tempered of course by your accountability to us. You see, at all times, so to speak, you must remember that we are selling this country to Americans . . .

CHENAYE   And Europeans . . .

XABA   The world, in fact.

CHENAYE   You see there is often bad press and other brand image erosion that impacts in a retrograde way on the consumer confidence of our putative target market which in turn creates the perception that South Africa has negative capabilities as an investment and is in fact . . .

XABA   Dangerous.

CHENAYE   You took the word out of my mouth.

XABA   So Chenaye, I can call you Chenaye.

CHENAYE   Of course, Mr Xaba, of course.

XABA   You must call me Mqeqeshe.

CHENAYE   Oh, I will, I will.

XABA   Chenaye and I were talking earlier over a bottle of wine. She introduced me to sushi made by a Zulu. You know, in fact, that we have joined the global village when you see a Zulu man is eating raw fish.

CHENAYE   And we came up with a rather exciting idea, didn't we? Well, actually, it was Mr Xaba's, at least Mqeqeshe's suggestion (*She struggles to pronounce 'Mqeqeshe's*). And that is, if we are selling our country, we have to include our most well known product somewhere in this campaign.

XABA   And that is, of course, Madiba.

CHENAYE   Exactly. Nelson Mandela.

Chenaye and Xaba switch to Kenneth and Mto.

MTO   Nelson Mandela?

KENNETH   No, I can see it working. I already see where we can go with this. Nelson Mandela, one of the great lions of Africa, the grand old lion of the liberation struggle, leading the young lions into the African Renaissance.

Kenneth and Mto switch to Chenaye and Xaba.

XABA   Sorry people, this may sound strange coming from a politician, like myself. But for this campaign, we don't want politics as such.

CHENAYE   You see, we can't sell South Africa with Mandela the revolutionary. It's just too . . . 1994.

45

XABA   We need, in fact, Mandela, the father of the nation.

CHENAYE   Even a step further than that, perhaps. Mandela the grandfather. Surrounded by a rainbow of children.

XABA   And my experience with international interest in South Africa, tells me that we've got to have the wildlife. We need to give the world a picture of Africa that they recognise and feel familiar with.

CHENAYE   Of course. Of course. I'm seeing elephants trumpeting at the sun.

XABA   Table Mountain with a lion in a tree.

Chenaye and Mto switch to Kenneth and Mto.

KENNETH   A lion in a tree?

Kenneth starts laughing uncontrollably.

MTO   Kenneth, I think we get the general idea. We need a wildlife scene. Lions, trees, bushveld.

Mto and Kenneth switch to Chenaye and Xaba.

CHENAYE (*Seething*)   Mr Xaba, I don't think we should waste any more of your time, we need to get you back to the airport. If you'll just give me a moment with my actors. Thank you, I'll be with you now.

Xaba becomes Mto.

CHENAYE (*To Mto and the now invisible Kenneth*)   If the client wants a lion in a tree, we don't laugh, we nod our heads. Then we give him a leopard in a tree and a lion at a watering hole. Then we throw in Table Mountain and we decorate it with Zulu dancers in skins and ostrich feathers. And muscles, not fat stomachs and flabby chests. And if he wants them all to sing The Lion Sleeps Tonight, or highlights from Ipi Tombi, or Hold Him Down You Zulu Warrior, then we give him that as well. And I don't think you understand that, Kenneth. You're off the project. Mto, I'll call you. Soon.

SCENE ELEVEN

Mto's backyard

Kenneth is half-heartedly rummaging through a box. Mto is standing to one side. Uncomfortable.

MTO   I'm pretty sure that's everything.

KENNETH   No, it isn't. I had a Zulu shield.

MTO   We didn't use a Zulu shield.

KENNETH   It's one of the props I brought in the beginning. When we were still exploring my ideas.

MTO   You mean that funny little souvenir thing? You want that?

Kenneth just stares at him.

MTO   OK, I'll check, it might be in the garage.

Mto leaves and becomes Prudence. Prudence is gardening and singing to herself.

PRUDENCE   Master Kenneth, you are going?

KENNETH   Yes Lahliwe.

PRUDENCE   When you are coming back?

KENNETH   Never.

PRUDENCE   Oh.

KENNETH   I've been sold for fifty pieces of silver, like with Judas.

PRUDENCE   Thirty.

KENNETH   What?

PRUDENCE   Judas was having thirty pieces of silver.

KENNETH   Either way Lahliwe, we are the meek, and the meek will inherit bugger all.

PRUDENCE   Sorry Master?

KENNETH   Ag, I'm just warning you – watch your back. Judas is all around us.

PRUDENCE   Devil. uSathane. Hawu Mntanami, we must always be watching for uSathane.

KENNETH   Don't get too comfortable here, Lahliwe.

PRUDENCE   Sorry?

KENNETH   Maybe Mto will change his mind.

PRUDENCE   He is a good boy. He gives me a garden.

KENNETH   The Lord giveth and the Lord taketh away.

PRUDENCE   Amen.

KENNETH   Don't count on him. That's your house, not this one. You must plant your garden there.

PRUDENCE   Master Jimmy only wants grass. Just nice grass with the lawnmower.

KENNETH   Lahliwe, you don't ask, you don't get, I know. Tell you what, I'll ask him for you. Hey Jimmy! You there?

PRUDENCE   Hayi, hayi, hayi, hayi, hayi!

KENNETH   OK, OK, don't worry. I won't say a thing.

Prudence becomes Mto.

MTO   Kwenzenjani lapha, Ma? Hey Kenneth, what's all the shouting about? Why is she upset?

KENNETH   Just warning her about putting all her eggs in one basket. Snakes in the grass, you know. And Jimmy's right: the grass is a bit long on this side of the fence. Well, I've got my things. I guess I'm out of here.

MTO   Come on Kenneth, don't be like that. I got us a chicken curry bunny chow. Share it with me.

KENNETH   Break some bread? A last supper? I don't think so.

MTO   Kenneth, don't be a fucking martyr. You will live.

KENNETH   Let me get this right. They want my ideas, but they don't want me?

MTO   They don't want our ideas either.

KENNETH   No, I said my ideas. What I wanted us to do in the first place is what they want. Singing and dancing. I told you. You don't get it, do you? They want a face, not a brain. And all of a sudden you don't mind being a happy native.

MTO   What's that supposed to mean?

KENNETH   Oh come on, Mto.

MTO   Maybe I'm a performer with the right talent for the job. Is that not another way of looking at it?

KENNETH   Ja whatever.

MTO   Are you saying I shouldn't do it?

KENNETH   Do it. It's money on a plate. Do it.

MTO   And I came into this thing, because you dangled it in front of me.

KENNETH   OK, OK.

MTO   Because I've got financial responsibilities here Kenneth. I don't like it, but I've got a house to pay off.

KENNETH   I know you've got a fucking house! House, car, contract, bum in the butter, 'a' for away, you've got it all broer! Your father was a hero of the struggle, what can I say? You're a Zulu, Samurai, rainbow, renaissance, previously disadvantaged, affirmative fucking warrior! I can't compete, you win, a hundred nil!

MTO   Fuck off, Kenneth! Fuck the hell off!

KENNETH   You said it!

A pause.

MTO   So, what are you going to do?

KENNETH   I'm going to fuck the hell off. Back to London. Earn real money: Pounds.

MTO   How?

KENNETH   Ancestral visa. My grandfather was British. Three years there and I become a British citizen.

MTO   Is that all it takes? You lose one job and you're running for your passport. What is this place? A sinking ship? Everyone's running.

KENNETH   I'm not running, I'm being pushed. Losing this job is the writing on the wall. It's telling me something.

MTO   What? That you can't live in a country run by blacks?

KENNETH   It's not that simple. I'm tired of playing the game. It's all bullshit. Affirmative action bullshit. I'm sick of apologising for being the wrong colour.

Mto laughs.

KENNETH   What?

MTO   I'm sorry Kenneth. I'm very, very sorry. You want me to apologise for being the right colour? Apologise for having the right father? Should I apologise for pissing in my pants when the cops came looking for him? Should I apologise for hating my father when my mother worked herself to death? Should I apologise for seeing burnt bodies whenever I look at a car tyre? Should I apologise for getting a job that you didn't; not because I'm better than you, but because I'm blacker? No!

Mto watches him go. Kenneth becomes Jimmy.

JIMMY   Jeez, I thought the show was over.

MTO   It is.

JIMMY   So now is this a new one?

MTO   No, it's over Jimmy.

A pause.

JIMMY   Look, the other day. Calling the cops. I . . . overreacted.

MTO   Yes, you did.

A pause.

JIMMY   I see Prudence has been doing some gardening.

MTO   Yes.

JIMMY   I know you think I'm a bit funny, not letting her plant in my yard.

MTO   Oh, I don't think it's funny at all.

JIMMY   It's just . . . I have my reasons, you know. Those squatters stripped her last garden bare. They see a garden in my yard they're going to be sneaking in here whenever I turn my back. I've seen them, looking over your wall. I'm telling you, you're going to have trouble.

MTO   Like you did.

A pause.

MTO   Maybe you should join Terry.

JIMMY   Hey?

MTO   If things are so bad here, you should go. Join Terry Rushbrooke, over in England.

JIMMY   Oh. When you said Terry, I thought you meant . . .

MTO   What?

JIMMY   Terrorist. We used to call them terries. For short. When I was in the army.

MTO   Was that before or after you cut their ears off?

JIMMY   No man, I never . . . oh, pulling my leg.

MTO   No.

JIMMY   Anyway, I'll keep an eye on things. Make sure none of them jump your fence to steal pumpkins.

MTO   As long as you shoot to kill. The only good squatter's a dead squatter.

A pause.

JIMMY   See the grass is getting a bit long there. I could mow it this afternoon, if you like.

MTO   No, that won't be necessary.

JIMMY   Oh. You bought yourself a lawn-mower?

MTO   No. I'm letting the grass grow.

JIMMY   What for?

MTO   So the goats have something to eat.

JIMMY   Goats?

MTO   I've decided I'm going to keep a few goats in my yard. It's a Zulu thing. We think it's part of living in Africa. We're funny that way.

JIMMY   OK, I see. Chip on the shoulder. I didn't think you had one. I thought you were different.

MTO   One of the good ones? No, not me.

JIMMY   Get yourself a few goats. It'll fit in perfectly with the rest of your 'African' farm. But you can find yourself a new labourer.

MTO   I don't need a labourer. I'm letting the grass grow.

JIMMY   I'm not talking about me, you cheeky shit. I'm talking about Prudence. You can get someone else to grow your pumpkins and mielies. (*To Prudence, who is apparently gardening*) Prudence. You're finished here, Mto doesn't need you any more.

MTO   That garden is not mine. It belongs to Prudence.

JIMMY   So what's this then? The local black club. Looking after each other.

MTO   No. It's just me showing an old lady some respect. Not that I owe it to her. She's never wiped my arse.

JIMMY   You fucking . . .

MTO   Say it. Go on say it.

JIMMY   You just need to mind your own business. You want to be the big chief of the secret black club, that's your problem. Fill the yard with goats, cows, whatever. Who gives a shit? Let it go like the rest of Africa. Because I've seen it. In the army. I didn't cut ears off terrorists, like you think I did. I didn't kick down doors in the townships. I did border patrol.

We'd see them coming towards us. Blacks from Mozambique. And we'd come out at them, rifles cocked, always expecting one of them to have a grenade or an AK47. But they just had shit. Bundles of shit. Herbs and empty jam tins and fucked-up old blankets. And we'd put them and all their useless shit on a truck and send them home again. But they'd always come back. Keep trying until they got through or until they were killed by lions, or drowned in a river. And even though they were all half-starved and fucked up, arms and legs missing from the landmines, we still lost. We had guns, but they had numbers. That's what's happening. That squatter camp – it's a war we can never win. People who walk through lions are desperate. Too desperate . . .

MTO (*Interrupting*)   Desperate? So desperate they killed your wife and left the gun behind?

JIMMY   Don't fuck with me.

MTO   Like we both know, Jimmy, all kaffirs are thieves. Why would they leave the gun behind?

Jimmy draws his gun. Mto becomes Prudence intervening.

PRUDENCE   Master Jimmy! Hayi, hayi, hayi, hayi, hayi. Wenzani? Master Jimmy.

JIMMY   Stay out of this Prudence.

PRUDENCE   No. This is bad. Bad thing will happen. You must stop to use gun.

JIMMY   Piss off, Prudence!

PRUDENCE   Master Jimmy. Leave gun. (*She moves to take the gun from him*)

JIMMY   What do you think you're doing? I'm not going to waste a bullet on this piece of shit. If you want to scratch around in his garden like one of those squatter camp savages, you can. Go! And don't come back! (*To Mto*) She's all yours. (*He turns to go*) One good kaffir deserves another. You're a kaffir! So fuck off, you're fired!

PRUDENCE   Jimmy!

Startled by the change in her tone, Jimmy turns back.

PRUDENCE   Little boy Jimmy. Little boy Jimmy never call me kaffir. Even Baas Louw, your father, never call me kaffir. That is devil talking. uSathane. Me, I am Ma Sibisi. Me, I am oldest woman for Sibisi family from Maphumulo. I am holy woman in Zionist church. I am president of the Hallelujah Jehovah Funeral and Saving Society. I am not kaffir. You do not tell me to go. I am here forty years, I am here to this house. Before you was born, I am here for your father and your mother. Your parents, who you never pray for them. I pray to God every day for your mother and your father, because you do never pray for them. Because I am not kaffir. Because now, I am your mother. Every day I pray for you. And I pray for Anna, your wife. I pray for her because she is dead, because she is also my daughter like you are my son.

SCENE TWELVE

In the lounge of Mto's house

CHENAYE   Sorry I'm late.

MTO   No that's fine. African time, you know. I'm used to it.

CHENAYE   Oh you! So, this is your little house. I love what you've done with it.

MTO   Well, we try.

CHENAYE   Very African. But nice. Really quaint. Are those Zulu masks?

MTO   Indonesian.

CHENAYE   Ooh. Such cosmopolitan tastes. And who is this handsome man?

MTO   My father.

CHENAYE   Oh right. That play you wrote. You must be so proud of him.

MTO   What makes you say that?

CHENAYE   Well, I mean . . . the struggle . . . he was a freedom fighter wasn't he?

MTO   He was a guerrilla.

CHENAYE   But he did fight for freedom.

MTO   Did he?

CHENAYE   We're a free country now, because of Mandela, and people like your father.

MTO   So back in the eighties, when bombs went off in shopping centres, is that what you all said here in the white suburbs? 'We're one step closer to freedom.'

CHENAYE   But your play . . .

MTO   Artistic license. To be honest, I didn't really know my father. All I know is he went away when I was very small, and then one day he planted a bomb in a shopping centre.

CHENAYE   Oh. Really.

MTO   Don't worry. He didn't kill anyone, except himself. He got it wrong, you see. Detonated it by accident. What my neighbour would call a stupid kaffir.

CHENAYE   You don't mean that. My Zulu teacher told us that Zulu's always respect the amadlosi.

MTO   No, you're right. That's what my neighbour would say, not me. Here, smell this. Umhlwehlwe.

CHENAYE   Umhlwehlwe? So what's it for.

MTO   I burn it with incense. It's how I communicate with my father, even if he wasn't really a father, or a hero. It's ironic though: they tell me he was a Marxist and an atheist. That he said it was all superstition, that Zulu stuff. 'The opiate of the masses.'

CHENAYE   So this is like a plant?

MTO   No actually. It's dried offal, from a slaughtered goat.

CHENAYE   Umhlwehlwe. Nice word. See, I've been working really hard at my Zulu. It is just such a beautiful language, isn't it? We've learnt some idioms. 'Izandla ziyagezana.'

MTO   'One hand washes the other.'

CHENAYE   Yes. I use it now whenever I get a new black client. You wash my hands, I'll wash yours. I mean let's face it hey. That's where the market is. The black market. Not the 'black' market, obviously, I mean . . . (*Looking out a window*) Oh, look! It's that white gardener you told me about. With the gun. Does he work for your neighbour too?

MTO   No, I was kidding. Pulling your leg. He is my neighbour.

CHENAYE   And he mows your lawn?

MTO   No, not any more. I bought my own lawn-mower. Quite enjoy cutting the grass. There's something almost therapeutic about it. Like meditation.

CHENAYE   I know what you mean. Mindless. I'm like that with painting my nails. So what is he doing then?

MTO   It's a long story, but the short version is that he's moving his maid's garden.

CHENAYE   Moving her garden?

MTO   Yes, she planted it somewhere else, and now he's letting her plant it in his yard.

CHENAYE   And he's doing the work himself?

MTO   Yes.

CHENAYE   Isn't that sweet, hey? You know it's the new South Africa when you see signs of hope like that. He must be a nice guy.

MTO   No, he's a screwed up arsehole. We don't even talk to each other. Jimmy's not ever coming home again.

CHENAYE   But isn't that his house? Is he moving?

MTO   No, but he's on border patrol, for the rest of his life. He's been out there for years, waiting for the barbarians.

CHENAYE   I know the type. Dinosaurs. It's adapt or die, isn't it?

MTO   So, you're an adapter?

CHENAYE   Aren't we all?

MTO   I suppose we are. I got us some lunch. Are you hungry?

CHENAYE   What is it?

MTO   Well, I was going to get you some real working-class Zulu food. You know, 'warts and all', from the street. Walkie Talkies.

CHENAYE   Sounds wonderful. Walkie Talkies?

MTO   Boiled chicken. Heads and feet.

CHENAYE   Well, um . . .

MTO   Don't worry. I decided to give you some traditional Durban food instead. Bunny chow. I hope you eat with your hands.

CHENAYE   Perhaps we should get to business first.

MTO   OK.

CHENAYE   So, are you still coming on board?

MTO   Yes.

CHENAYE   I am so relieved. I thought you were calling me here to pull out. Now, we've got a new writer I'd love you to meet. I think he's going to be perfect for the job. His ideas are marvellous.

MTO   That's what I wanted to talk to you about. I don't think we'll need your writer.

CHENAYE   You don't? Why, do you have someone in mind?

MTO   I'd like to write it.

CHENAYE   You?

MTO   Yes.

CHENAYE   Look, this is a big project and I have to say that . . .

MTO   Chenaye, if I don't get to write it, then I'm out.

A pause.

CHENAYE   OK. So what's your idea.

MTO   It's about a seed.

CHENAYE   A seed?

MTO   And an old woman.

CHENAYE   She's black, I hope?

MTO   She's black.

CHENAYE   Ah. I'm seeing it. I'm seeing it. Mother Africa planting the seed of the African Renaissance.

MTO   No. She's not Mother Africa. She's an old black woman.

CHENAYE   Just an old black woman.

MTO   Not just an old black woman. She grows pumpkins the size of car tyres. And she's the head of the Sibisi clan in Maphumulo. And she's the president of the Hallelujah Jehovah Funeral and Saving Society.

CHENAYE   OK, OK. I'm seeing something we can work with. But now I'm thinking 'more visual'. Give the potential investors some nice positive images. Now the Zulu dancers, would they . . .

MTO   No Zulu dancers.

CHENAYE   No Zulu dancers?

MTO   No.

CHENAYE   Gumboot dancers?

MTO   No gumboot dancers. No happy natives jumping up and down. It begins with an old black woman planting a seed. And it ends with a squatter camp covered in pumpkins.

END